STORIES FROM ANCIENT CIVILISATIONS

Greece

STORIES FROM ANCIENT CIVILISATIONS

Greece

Shahrukh Husain
Illustrated by Bee Willey

Evans

Introduction

Myths are probably the earliest stories ever told. People in ancient times used them to explain all that was important in life, like how the universe was created and how the stars, sun, moon and planets appeared in the sky. To them these elements were gods, who they worshipped and who they believed controlled their lives. If the gods were kept happy, they would be kind to the people.

Myths are usually about important matters like birth, death and the afterlife, and tend to have a moral. The story of Eurynome tells us how the ancient Greeks believed sinners would be sent to a dark place far underground called Tartarus to be punished. Other myths show that we go to the Underworld after death. The heroic tales, such as the story of Theseus and the Minotaur, show how the most difficult problems can be solved if we refuse to accept failure and use both strength and intelligence to help us.

People in ancient Greece often travelled huge distances, searching for food and shelter. Some were warlike and went to conquer rich and fertile lands. These conquerors brought their own gods with them. When they settled somewhere new, an exchange took place. They introduced their gods to the local people and in turn began to worship some of theirs. Sometimes the same gods were called by different names, as old stories blended with new ones. For example, the early Greeks called their sea god Oceanus and their sun god Helios, while later they became known as Poseidon and Apollo.

Greek-speaking people existed as long ago as 2200-2100 BCE. Their civilisations had disappeared by the time ancestors of the present day Greek nations came to power. But from the earliest times, Greek myths have mainly been about gods, kings, heroes and magical animals. The gods are all-powerful and like to use humans to amuse themselves. Heroes are brave men, usually the sons of gods, and they are often up against wicked kings who have seized their thrones and send them on dangerous quests, hoping they will be killed by the monsters they have to combat.

All these myths were eventually written down as hymns and stories. The most famous of them are the epics of Hesiod (circa 700 BCE) and Homer (750-725 BCE) and the plays of Euripedes (455-408 BCE). It is important to remember that the gods in these stories were once as seriously worshipped by people as many people worship their own gods today.

For Florence Mae Wilson – S.H

First published in paperback in 2008 by Evans Brothers Limited
2A Portman Mansions
Chiltern Street
London W1U 6NR

Printed in China by WKT Co. Ltd

British Library Cataloguing in Publication Data
Husain, Shahrukh
    Stories from Ancient Civilisations: Greece. - (Stories from ancient civilisations)
    1. Mythology, Greek - Juvenile literature
    2. Greece - Civilization - To 146 B.C - Juvenile literature
    I.Title
    398.2'0938
    ISBN 978 0 237 53603 9

CREDITS
Series Editor: Louise John
Editor: Julia Bird
Design: Robert Walster
Artworks: Bee Willey
Production: Jenny Mulvanny

VISIT OUR WEBSITE
Evans
www.evansbooks.co.uk

Contents

Eurynome

This story is about the beginning of time and the creation of the world. It reflects the ancient Greek belief that any creature - man, bird or beast - who claimed to be able to match the achievements of the gods was committing a terrible sin, and had to be severely punished for it.

The Greeks believed that a hammer dropped from the Underworld (where the dead lived) would take ten days to reach Tartarus. It was guarded by three one-eyed giants called Cyclopes and covered with roots from Earth and sea. Gods and monsters were sent there to be punished for their sins and were terrified of being imprisoned in its darkness forever.

LONG AGO, WHEN LITTLE EXISTED EXCEPT THE YAWNING LABYSS, EURYNOME ROSE OUT OF DARKNESS AND DISORDER. For a long time she wandered alone, floating on the waves. Then she decided to rest. But she could find no solid space on which to place her feet.

'I will drag earth from out of the sea to make solid ground,' Eurynome decided. She spun around in a wild dance on the waves, whipping up a wind. She held out her arms, trying to catch the wind between her palms, and from her movements, she formed a mighty python.

'I'll call you Ophion,' she announced.

Eurynome danced on until at last it was time to create the universe.

'I will turn myself into a dove,' she said. After brooding on the waves, she laid the universal egg.

'Coil yourself seven times around this egg and keep it warm until it hatches,' she commanded Ophion.

Ophion did as she asked. Finally, the egg split in two. Ophion and Eurynome watched in wonder as the glowing planets spilled out of the egg and took their places in the sky. Eurynome and Ophion settled peacefully on Mount Olympus. They watched the earth hanging in its orbit, slowly filling with rivers and mountains, trees and plants, birds and animals.

Then, one day Ophion boasted, 'How clever I was to create the universe.'

'I created the universe,' Eurynome stormed. 'Not you.'

But Ophion kept arguing. 'All you did was lay an

egg. Any bird can do that.'

Eurynome flew into an immense rage and kicked out at Ophion. The mighty serpent reared up at her. Eurynome lashed out again, knocking Ophion's teeth out of his snarling head.

'Go to Tartarus,' she ordered. 'It is the deepest, darkest place in the universe. You will live there forever with the monsters and other evil creatures.'

Ophion let out a mighty shriek and disappeared, leaving Eurynome alone on Mount Olympus.

'Now I shall create a cluster of seven planets,' she decided, 'and giant gods to guard each one.'

When that was done, Eurynome created the first man and named him Pelasgus.

Mount Olympus is the highest and most famous mountain in Greece. According to Greek mythology, it was where the twelve greatest gods, including Zeus, the chief god, lived (see page 13). These gods became known as the Olympians.

Gaia the Earth

This story is about good and evil actions, and how these can change the world. It shows how it is sometimes necessary for a good person to take action against an evil one – as Cronus did against Uranus – to make sure that the force of good triumphs.

Gaia, the Earth, was the solid ground of the universe. But she was lonely.

'I will create a partner as big and strong as myself,' she said. Concentrating hard, she formed Uranus, the sky, who became her constant companion.

Gaia was happy now. Every night, when darkness fell Uranus would come down to her and they would spend many hours together. Gaia soon gave birth to her first children, Oceanus and Tethys. Many others followed. These children were called the Titans.

Suddenly, Gaia had many beings to love and Uranus was jealous.

'I will get rid of them,' he decided. 'Then I can have Gaia all to myself again.'

That night when Uranus visited Gaia, he seized her children and buried them in her body, which was by now covered with mountains and valleys and streams. Soon, Gaia had more children. Five more pairs of Titans followed and there were others besides: the three Cyclopes, who were named after thunder and lightning, and the Hecatoncheires who were giants with a hundred arms each. Each Titan couple gave birth to more children and the universe was blessed with light, stars, sun, moon, planets and many other wonderful things. But every night when Uranus came to visit, he would bury a few more of Gaia's children in her body.

Gaia's body grew heavy and she groaned and twisted with her massive burden. At last, she could bear it no more. She reached into her body, which was the Earth, and pulled out iron to make a sharp, curved blade studded with spikes. Then she called her remaining children together.

'Uranus has committed the first evil deed,' she told them. 'Evil must be punished. Which of you has the courage to punish him and free the rest?'

No one said a word. Then suddenly, Cronus echoed her words.

'Uranus has committed the first evil deed. I am brave enough to punish him and free my brothers and sisters.'

Gaia smiled warmly at him. She held up the weapon she had made.

'This is a scythe,' she explained. 'Hide near me tonight. When Uranus comes, strike him with it.'

That night, Cronus hid in a cave until Uranus was deep in conversation. Then he crept out and struck Uranus hard. With a bellow, Uranus the sky drew away from Gaia the Earth and fled roaring to the distant horizon where he stayed for all eternity. A few drops of his blood fell into the sea to form Aphrodite, goddess of beauty and love.

Together, Gaia and Cronus freed the others and, as a reward for his courage, Gaia made Cronus king of all the gods.

How Zeus came to Power

This story is about the first war and how wars begin. When kings think of themselves instead of their people, as Cronus did, they must be overthrown and this often leads to war. Some people believe that this story is based on a real war that took place a long time before history was written down.

EVERYTHING SEEMED PERFECT IN THE KINGDOM OF CRONUS AND HIS WIFE RHEA. But deep inside, Cronus was troubled. He had once been told that a child of his would take his place as king.

'If all my children die,' he thought to himself, 'I can rule forever.'

So every time Rhea gave birth, he opened his mouth and swallowed the baby whole.

'Stop this,' Rhea pleaded with him. 'You're becoming as evil as your father, Uranus.'

But Cronus refused to listen. So the next time Rhea was going to have a baby, she prayed to Gaia for help.

'Take the child to Lyktos, in Crete,' Gaia told her. 'I'll meet you there.'

Rhea crept away in the dark of night and gave birth to her son in a cave. Gaia took the child and Rhea returned to her husband.

'Where is the new child?' Cronus asked.
Rhea handed him a stone wrapped in a blanket and
Cronus swallowed it. Baby Zeus was safe.

Zeus grew faster than any being before him. Soon, he
learned about war and wisdom. When Zeus was ready,
Gaia persuaded Cronus to meet him.

Zeus bowed deeply before his father. He was
charming and respectful and glowed with a golden light.

'May I offer you a small gift?' he asked. 'It is a
remarkable herb that was given to me by a goddess.'

Carefully, Cronus examined the food which Zeus
was holding out. It looked harmless, so he swallowed
it. Immediately, his stomach churned and he
began to vomit.

Zeus grew up in the forest, hidden away from his father, and was nursed by a nymph called Amalthea, who took the form of a goat. He was protected by a magical goatskin cloak which, along with the thunderbolt he carried, became a symbol of his godliness.

11

Out came the stone he had eaten instead of Zeus. Next followed the goddesses Hestia, Demeter and Hera, then the gods, Poseidon and Hades. Led by Zeus, they surrounded their father.

'This is the end for you,' Zeus announced. 'I banish you from heaven. I will rule in your place.'

A thunderous noise interrupted Zeus. The Titans had discovered that their brother Cronus was in trouble. They had not forgotten that he had bravely rescued them from Uranus. In an instant they strode to Mount Olympus, ready to defend him.

The three Hecatoncheires were giants with a hundred arms and fifty heads and the three Cyclopes were master craftsmen, with one eye each in their foreheads. Cronus, their brother, sent them to Tartarus after he was warned that they would eventually help to overthrow his rule.

Zeus and his brothers and sisters fought back. Both groups were strong fighters and the war raged on for ten long years. Finally, Gaia decided to put an end to it.

'Release the Cyclopes and the Hecatoncheires from Tartarus,' Gaia told Zeus. 'Strengthen them with nectar and ambrosia, the food of the gods. Then make them fight the Titans.'

Zeus, Poseidon and Hades entered Tartarus and found the mighty creatures in chains. With a powerful blow, Zeus released them. They promised to fight with Zeus against the Titans and awarded each of the gods special weapons against evil. To Hades, they gave a magic helmet which made him invisible. To Poseidon, they gave an enormous trident - one shake of it could make the Earth and sea shudder and tremble. Zeus was given thunder and lightning bolts.

This time, with the help of the Cyclopes and the Hecatoncheires, the Olympians defeated the Titans. Zeus carried his father Cronus off to the Isle of the Blessed, where he left him to rule forever from the Tower of Cronus.

'From this day on,' said Gaia to Zeus, 'you will be leader of the gods and king of heaven and Earth.'

Zeus remembered his brothers had helped him. He decided to thank them.

'I will give the Underworld to Hades,' he said. 'From there he will make sure that justice is done. And Poseidon will be called the 'Earth-Shaker', master of earthquakes and the oceans and all that is in them.'

Gods and Goddesses of Mount Olympus

Cronus - *youngest of the twelve Titans created by Gaia*

Aphrodite
goddess of beauty and love

Hestia
goddess of the home and the fireplace

Demeter
goddess of the Earth

Zeus
chief god and god of thunder, lightning and storms

Hera
Zeus' wife and sister, goddess of marriage and women

Poseidon
god of the sea and earthquakes

Hades
god of the Underworld

Persephone
daughter of Zeus and Demeter and queen of the Underworld

Ares
son of Zeus and Hera and god of war

Hephaistos
son of Zeus and Hera and blacksmith of the gods

Artemis
daughter of Zeus, twin sister of Apollo and goddess of the hunt

Apollo
son of Zeus and god of music, poetry and the sun

Hermes
son of Zeus and messenger of the gods

Athena
daughter of Zeus and goddess of war and wisdom

13

Heroes and Magical Animals

These three stories about heroes and magical animals are taken from a group of Greek classical myths, known as cycles. Each cycle recounts the experiences and adventures of one famous hero and shows how they use their intelligence and cunning to defeat fearsome enemies. This story is about the hero Hercules.

Some say Cerberus had three or four heads, others that he had fifty. A bristling ridge of fur ran down the centre of his back. Snakes grew, wriggling and writhing, from his tail and his shaggy belly.

Hercules and the Hound of Hell

THE GREAT HERO HERCULES STOOD BEFORE HIS COUSIN, KING EURYSTHEUS. The king had set him twelve tasks before he would let him come to live in his homeland of Argos. Many brave men had died trying to fulfil the tasks, but Hercules had already completed eleven of them. Now Eurystheus revealed the deadliest task of all.

'Bring me Cerberus, the hound of hell from Hades.'

'But the living aren't allowed to enter the Underworld!' Hercules exclaimed, shocked. 'And no one ever comes back from it. That's why it's called the Land of the Dead.'

'That,' replied the king smugly, 'is your problem to resolve, not mine.'

So Hercules set off across the great river Styx which divided the land of the dead from the world of the living. As the boat drifted to the shore, Hercules caught sight of Cerberus guarding the gates of the Underworld. He was no ordinary dog. His many heads snapped and growled and his eyes flashed blue fire like massive sparks from a flint. As the hound's ferocious barks reached his ears, Hercules thought hard how to conquer him. But as he climbed out of the boat, Cerberus recognised the hero and began to run. Hercules chased after him, until at last they reached the thrones of Hades and Persephone.

'Mighty king and queen,' Hercules greeted them. 'Please allow me to take Cerberus back to Earth to complete the last of my twelve quests.'

'If you can capture him with no weapon,' Hades mocked, 'take him.'

Hercules nodded, knowing this would be almost impossible. Cerberus bit him hard and lashed his tail back and forth. The snakes stung and poisoned Hercules, but he locked the beast in his great arms and held on with all his strength.

At last nearly all the breath was crushed from Cerberus. Hercules slipped a chain round the hound's neck and led him back across the Styx to Argos. The crowds, who had come to witness his triumph, cheered wildly. People could not believe that Hercules had returned alive from the Underworld. At last he was free to live in Argos.

In this very famous story, Theseus tackles the Minotaur of Crete in the labyrinth (maze) where the monster lived. Theseus was a great hero of Greek mythology and had many other exciting adventures.

Theseus and the Minotaur

ALL OF ATHENS WAS IN MOURNING. People crowded around King Minos of Crete, crying and beating their breasts in despair.

'What's the matter?' asked Theseus.

'Oh stranger,' replied a woman, sadly. 'Every nine years Minos takes seven young men and women from us to sacrifice to a monster who is half-man, half-bull.'

'The Minotaur!' Theseus exclaimed.

The woman nodded, tears running down her face.

Theseus pushed through the crowds to face Minos.

'Take me,' he demanded.

King Minos looked Theseus up and down.

'You're young and fit,' he chuckled.

'Get on the ship and prepare to die.'

Theseus joined the others on the boat and they set sail for Crete, where they were met by the priestess Ariadne.

'The Minotaur lives in a labyrinth,' she said. 'You will face it alone. If you come back alive, you may go home. But I must warn you that no one ever has before.'

Theseus thrust himself to the front. Ariadne saw his determination and courage.

'You look brave,' she whispered. 'Take this ball of twine. Fasten it to the entrance of the labyrinth and hold on to it. If you escape the Minotaur, follow it back out.'

Theseus thanked Ariadne and entered the dark cave. He walked on until he heard the sound of stamping and snorting. All at once, the monster was rushing at him, bellowing and rearing up. Theseus stepped aside, then attacked it from behind to avoid its deadly horns. A violent struggle followed. At times the Minotaur was winning; at others, Theseus.

The Greeks believed that sacrifices made the gods happy. They offered them sacrifices of grain, wine and honey, as well as animals on special feast days. If they wanted to please a monster, like the Minotaur, they sacrificed humans. They hoped the lives of others would be spared in return.

With the last of his strength, Theseus grasped the Minotaur's horns and wrestled him to the ground, then struck him with his sword. The great beast collapsed, howling. Swiftly Theseus turned, snatched up his twine and followed it out to the mouth of the labyrinth. Then he hid it out of sight so that Ariadne would not be in trouble.

Outside, the crowd stood in disbelieving silence. Theseus really was a hero. The young people of Athens were safe once more.

This story shows how heroes, like Bellerophon, may have to rely on quick thinking to succeed in their quests. Greek heroes were often helped by the gods because they defended the forces of good against evil.

The Furies, Muses and Fates were goddess threesomes. The Furies made laws about right and wrong and punished wrong-doers, and the Muses ruled music, learning and poetry. The Fates decided people's destinies.

Bellerophon and the Chimaera

KING IOBATUS OF LYCIA WAS FURIOUS WITH HIS GUEST, BELLEROPHON. He had been told that Bellerophon had insulted his daughter.

'The Furies would punish me if I killed a guest in my kingdom,' Iobatus thought. So he hatched a clever plan.

'Go to Caria,' he commanded Bellerophon. 'My enemy, the King of Caria, has tamed a creature called the Chimaera. Kill it before he can use it against my people.'

Wisely, Bellerophon decided to ask the advice of a man who could see into the future.

'You must tame Pegasus, the winged horse,' the man told him. 'Sleep in the temple of Apollo tonight. If you are lucky, the gods will help you.'

That night, Bellerophon dreamt of the goddess Athena. 'No man can tame Pegasus,' she said. 'But show him this bridle and he will let you ride him.'

Bellerophon awoke holding a golden bridle and set off, searching everywhere. Eventually, he arrived in Corinth. Tired and thirsty, he stopped at a well. There, at last before him, stood a fabulous, winged horse.

Pegasus saw Bellerophon and spread his wings, ready to fly away. Swiftly, Bellerophon

held out Athena's bridle. Pegasus flicked his mane and came over, bowing his head for the bridle. Bellorophon leapt on to his back and together they flew to Caria.

The smoke from the Chimaera's fiery breath rose high above Caria. She was a hideous monster. Her lion head roared above the body of a goat and the hindquarters of a snake and she spat flames and poison. Bellerophon shot a stream of arrows at her, but they bounced off her thick hide like twigs. Then he had an idea. He loosened a piece of lead from the binding on his quiver and attached it to the point of his arrow. Carefully, he aimed into the mouth of the monster. The Chimaera caught the arrow and threw back her head to mock him. The next instant, the arrow was ablaze. The Chimaera shrieked in pain. The lead had melted and was pouring down her throat, choking and burning. Within moments, she lay dead.

Bellerophon stroked Pegasus' silky mane.

'Thank you, my friend,' he said. Then he and Pegasus flew back to Lycia, victorious.

The Greeks believed that gods spoke to them through people called oracles, who were usually priestesses. People went to oracles to ask for advice about the future. The answer came through dreams or the voice of a god. The temple where the priest or priestess was consulted was also known as an oracle.

Athena and Poseidon

This story describes how Athena, goddess of war, came to be the most important goddess of the people of Attica. After choosing Athena to be their patron, they won many wars and Attica eventually became an empire in its own right.

Athena sprang out of Zeus' head, clothed in a short cloak and golden armour. She carries a spear and a shield bearing the head of a fierce creature called the Gorgon Medusa, who had snakes for hair. Anyone who looked at the Medusa turned to stone. Poseidon is usually shown with a beard. He holds a three-pronged spear called a trident and the symbol of a fish links him to the sea.

LONG AGO, POSEIDON, GOD OF THE SEA AND ATHENA, GODDESS OF WAR, GOT INTO AN ARGUMENT. Each god claimed to be the patron deity of the kingdom of Attica. Their argument raged on for days.

At last, Athena who was also goddess of wisdom, said 'This is foolish. Let us decide by contest.'

So they went to King Cecrops who ruled Attica.

'We will each perform an act to benefit your kingdom,' they said. 'You will decide which is the greater. The winner will become your protector and patron god.'

Cecrops agreed and the contest began. Poseidon went first. He lifted his trident and brought it down on a rock with a resounding blow. Instantly, a jet of bubbling water gushed out, forming a large pool. Poseidon stood back, satisfied with his handiwork.

'Beat that,' he told Athena. 'A pond from a rock.'

Athena bent and planted a seed into the rock.

'This is my gift to Attica.' She touched the spot with her sceptre and a tree sprang up, its branches loaded with olives. 'Now, Cecrops, decide which gift is more special.'

Cecrops bowed his head. 'Causing water to flow from a rock shows great power,' he murmured. 'But the sea is visible all around dry land. This tree, on the other hand, is unique. Its fruit can be eaten and used to make oil for food and medicine. Athena's gift will be more useful.'

With a roar, Poseidon disappeared and Athena became the patron of Attica. A shrine was erected to honour her. And in time Attica became known as Athens after the goddess.

The Judgement of Paris

This story tells how the Trojan War was started. It was a long and terrible war between the Greeks and the Trojans, and many great heroes fought and died in it. It is described in the famous Greek epic by Homer called The Odyssey.

ERIS, GODDESS OF STRIFE, WAS ANGRY. Thetis, the daughter of Oceanus, was marrying King Peleas and all the gods of Mount Olympus were celebrating – except Eris. She had not been asked because she spread bad luck wherever she went.

'I'll teach them a lesson for insulting me,' she thought, throwing a golden apple among the guests. There was a hush when the apple landed. Then someone picked it up and read the message inscribed on it: 'For the most beautiful goddess.'

Three goddesses stepped forward, each holding out her hand. They were Hera, Aphrodite and Athena. Thetis and Peleas froze and their guests fell silent.

Eris laughed to herself.

'Whoever is chosen, the other two will be furious!'

The guests all turned to Zeus, the chief god, but he was too clever to get involved in the dispute. Hera and Athena were always quarrelling. And how would he explain to Aphrodite why he hadn't chosen her?

'Go to Mount Ida,' he ordered Hermes, the messenger god. 'Find a shepherd called Paris. He can decide.'

In a few moments, Hermes returned with Paris.

'Now, mortal,' Zeus commanded. 'You must decide who is the most beautiful goddess.'

Paris could hardly believe his ears. 'I'm just a shepherd boy. Please don't make me do this,' he pleaded. But the contest had begun.

'Choose me, Paris,' said Hera. 'I will make you ruler of all Asia.'

'Choose me,' said Athena, 'and you will be the wisest man on Earth.'

'Choose me,' said Aphrodite, 'and win the love of beautiful Helen of Troy.'

Without another thought, Paris made his judgement. 'All the goddesses are beautiful,' he said, bowing low. 'But I choose Aphrodite.'

High up in her dwelling, Eris chuckled wickedly to herself. She had laid the foundation for the biggest war the world had ever seen. Helen was married to the king of Troy, and when she ran away with Paris her husband came after them, starting a bitter war with Greece that would last many, many years.

The Greeks believed that the gods and goddesses had feelings like human beings. That is why Eris was jealous and the goddesses competed with each other just as humans might.

Apollo

This story is about the sun god Apollo, who was the son of Zeus. It shows us how Apollo came to be linked to the oracle at Delphi and emphasises the importance the Greeks placed on respecting holy places.

LETO, MOTHER OF APOLLO, WAS BEING CHASED BY TERRIFYING MONSTERS. She hid in a grove to give birth to Apollo and his twin sister Artemis. But soon she was on the run again. When Apollo was only four days old, he decided to get rid of the monsters for good.

'Make me a bow and plenty of arrows,' Apollo said to Hephaistos, the blacksmith of the gods.

Then Apollo set off on his journey to Mount Parnassus to find one of his mother's tormentors, a huge serpent

called Python. There, hiding in a cave beside a spring, he found the evil creature. He let fly a volley of arrows on the monster. Badly wounded, Python slithered away under the cover of the grass to the oracle in Delphi. He would be safe in the holy space of the oracle who had been given special powers by the gods.

Apollo knew that Python would not change his ways. He would get the oracle to heal him, then he would find Leto and hound her again. So Apollo fired more arrows at Python and this time he killed him.

'You have been violent in a sacred place!' thundered Zeus. 'Enter the temple now and cleanse yourself.'

Apollo knew his father was right but he was too frightened to face the oracle. Instead, he escaped across the sea to the kingdom of Crete. There he made his way to the king who said prayers to purify him.

Apollo was the sun god and is linked with healing, because the light and warmth that come from the sun ensure good health and growth. Because the sun can see everything from its place in the sky, Apollo is also linked with learning, especially music. His twin sister Artemis was the goddess of women and the hunt. Her shrine is at Ephesus.

Leto heard Apollo was in Crete and took Artemis to meet him there. As they walked together, they saw a beautiful grove and Leto stopped to pray. While she prayed, Apollo and Artemis explored their surroundings. Suddenly, they heard Leto screaming in terror and ran towards the grove. A giant was holding Leto high up in the air.

Together, the twins fastened their arrows to their bows and fired. The arrows pierced the giant and he fell to the ground.

'Anyone who tries to hurt my mother again,' declared Apollo, 'will be seeking his own death.'

Then Apollo returned to Delphi and built a temple there to make amends for his violence in the chamber of the oracle. From then on, the oracle at Delphi became Apollo's most famous temple.

The Kidnap of of Persephone

This story is about the seasons of the year. When Persephone returned to Earth, things began to grow again, which meant it was spring. Her eight-month stay lasted until the end of the summer. The four months of the year she spent in the Underworld were autumn, when plants wither and die, and winter, when there is very little growth.

In pictures, Demeter carries a sheaf of wheat or corn, a poppy, a sceptre or a flaring torch to show that she is the goddess of the Earth. She is also sometimes accompanied by snakes.

PERSEPHONE WAS PICKING FLOWERS. 'Mother will love these,' she smiled, enjoying their velvety touch and their jewel-like colours.

Suddenly, there was the thunder of hooves, and a rush of wind. The ground opened up beside Persephone. An arm shot out and snatched her.

'Mother!' Persephone screamed, as Hades, king of the Underworld, forced her into his carriage. Her mother, Demeter, ran to help her but the ground had closed up and there was no sign of Persephone.

Demeter disguised herself as an old woman and walked the world, looking for her daughter.

'Have you seen Persephone?' she asked Hesperus each night, as he let loose the stars into the sky. But he just shook his head sadly.

Every morning as Aurora brought the dawn, she asked 'Aurora, have you seen my daughter?' And Aurora looked at Demeter with pity and replied that she had not.

Demeter soon feared the worst. 'Night and day see everything on Earth and in heaven. If they can't see Persephone, she must be in the Underworld.'

Now, Demeter was the goddess of Earth and all that grows on it. So while she was sad, the world grew dark. Plants began to wither and die. Demeter sat on a large rock. For nine days and nights she sat still as if frozen with grief. On the tenth day, she heard a girl's voice:

'Why are you so sad?'

Demeter looked up. Standing before her was a little girl, holding her father's hand.

'I am Celeus,' the man said. 'Come to stay with us.'

Demeter accepted, explaining she would leave soon to find her daughter.

'I understand,' Celeus replied, sadly. 'My son Triptolemus is very ill. He may die soon.'

Later that night, Demeter secretly arose and fed Triptolemus a mixture of poppy juice and milk. Then she placed him gently on the warm ashes in the fireplace. As she did this, his mother came in. With a gasp, she snatched Triptolemus up.

'Why are you trying to hurt my son?' she cried. Then she saw Demeter shining in the full glory of a goddess.

'I was making Triptolemus immortal to thank you for your kindness,' said Demeter. 'You interrupted my spell, but I will reward you anyway. Your son will be healthy.' The bewildered mother watched Demeter draw a thick cloud around her and disappear.

Meanwhile, the gods were worried. 'Nothing grows in the wild or in the fields. The sun is so strong it singes everything. The rain vanishes altogether or falls so heavily that it drowns what is left. And all because Hades stole Persephone.'

Zeus spoke to Hades. 'If Demeter can't be with Persephone, Earth will be destroyed.'

'Persephone is my queen now,' Hades said cunningly. 'But I will obey you.'

Hades knew very well that Persephone could not return to Earth. The Fates had ruled that no one could leave the Underworld if they had eaten anything there. So Hades made sure Persephone had eaten a mouthful of pomegranate.

Zeus knew the Fates could not be ignored. Yet if Demeter and Persephone were not reunited, the Earth would surely die. An idea struck him.

'Persephone will stay in the Underworld for four months of each year. The rest, she will be with her mother,' he decreed.

Demeter was overjoyed to have Persephone back and all the while Persephone was with her, Earth was fertile and fruitful.

Glossary

ambrosia – a special substance belonging to the gods. It produced a heavenly fragrance.

Cerberus – a fearsome dog with many heads that guarded the gates to the Underworld.

Chimaera – a fire-breathing monster with the head of a lion, body of a goat and tail of a snake.

Crete – a large, mountainous island off the coast of the Greek mainland.

Cyclopes – the three giants who guarded the entrance to Tartarus. They each had one eye in the middle of their forehead.

deity – another name for a god or goddess.

Fates – the three goddesses responsible for controlling people's destinies.

fertile – used here to describe land or soil that contains lots of goodness, where plants and crops grow well.

Furies – the three goddesses who made laws about right and wrong and punished criminals.

Hecatoncheires – three giants, created by Gaia, who had a hundred arms and fifty heads each.

immortal – having everlasting life. An immortal being will never die.

labyrinth – a huge maze, such as the one built by King Minos of Crete to contain the Minotaur.

Minotaur – a monster, with the body of a man and head of a bull.

Mount Olympus – the highest mountain in Greece. According to Greek mythology, it was where the greatest gods lived.

Muses – the nine sister goddesses who looked after the arts, music and science.

mythology – the collection or study of myths.

nectar – a delicious drink, known as the drink of the gods.

Olympians – the name for the gods who lived on Mount Olympus.

oracle – a priest or priestess through whom the gods were believed to speak. People consulted them to ask questions about the future, and the answers could come in the voice of the god or in a dream. The temple at which the priest or priestess was consulted was also called an oracle.

patron god – the god or goddess who looked after and protected a kingdom, city or ruling family.

Pegasus – a beautiful winged horse, which was tamed by Bellerophon with a golden bridle given to him by the goddess Athena.

sacrifice – used here to describe the offering of food or drink to the gods. The Greeks believed that such gifts kept the gods happy. To monsters, such as the Minotaur, humans themselves were sometimes sacrificed, as people believed that the lives of others would be spared in return.

sin – breaking the command of a god.

Tartarus – a dark space far below the Underworld where wrongdoers were sent to be punished.

Titans – the name for the pairs of giant gods created by Eurynome to guard the sun, moon and planets. It was also the name for the sons and daughters of Gaia (the Earth) and Uranus (the sky).

Trojan War – a mighty war fought between the Greeks and the Trojans (people of Troy). It lasted ten years and ended with the destruction of the city of Troy.

Underworld – the world of the dead, where people go after they have died in the human world. It was also known as Hades, after the god of the Underworld.

Universe – space, where the sun, moon and planets are placed.

Index